Collins

Cascade 1

A SKILL-BASED COURSE IN ENVIRONMENTAL STUDIES

Series Editor
Padmini Sriraman

Components of DigiSuite

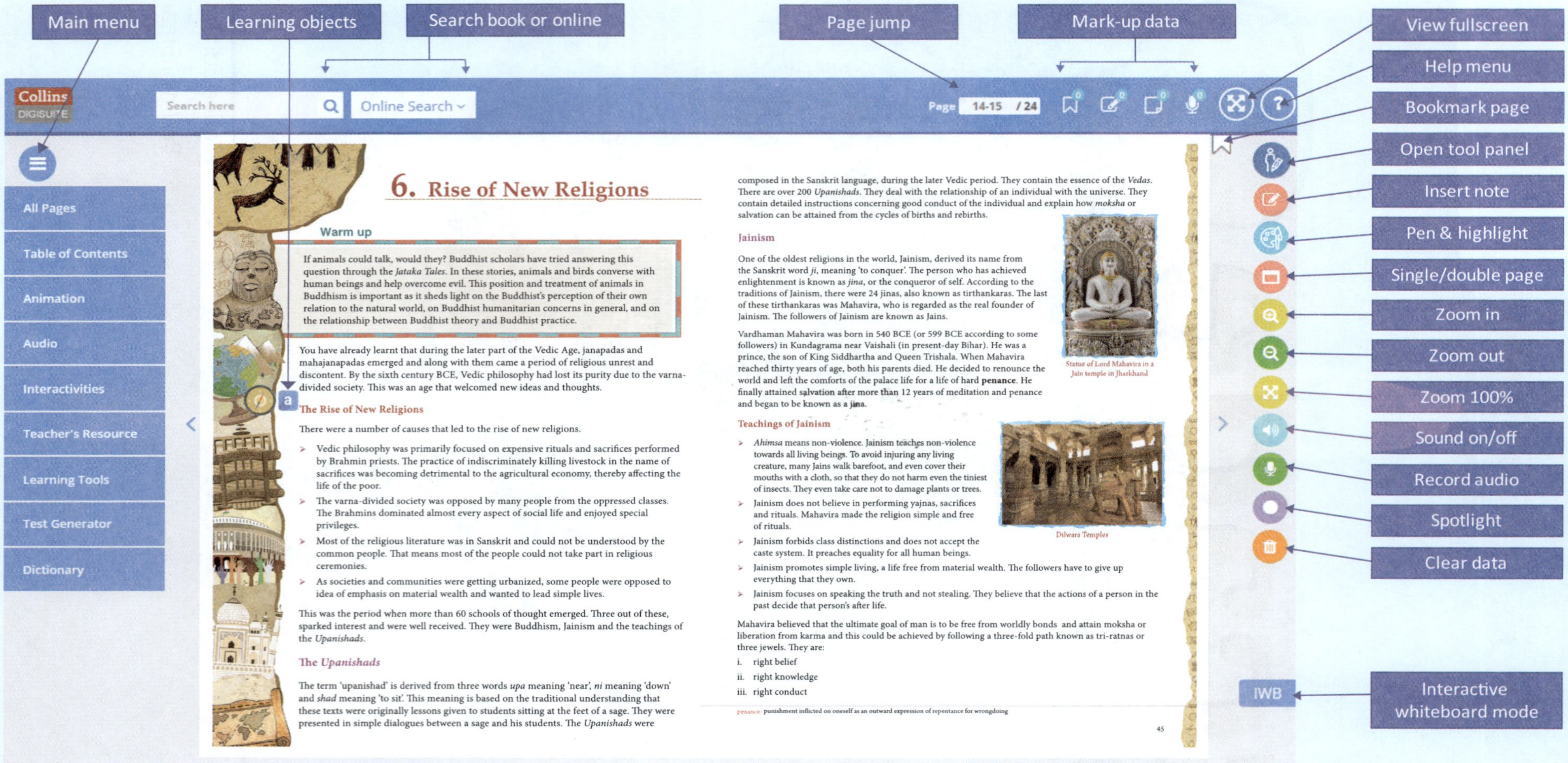

Student + Teacher

- **a** animations
- **ilt** instructor-led tutorials
- **ia** activities
- **w** worksheets
- audio
- **g** games
- **v** videos

Teacher-only

- **lp** lesson plans
- **w** worksheets
- **tn** teacher's notes
- **ak** answer keys

Preface

Cascade is a skill-based course on Environmental Studies and Social Studies for the foundational, preparatory and middle stages. This series for classes 1 to 8 is aligned to the National Education Policy, 2020. Taking into account the multidisciplinary nature of Environmental Studies and Social Studies, the series follows an interactive approach through a variety of tasks and stimulating content. This series deals with the study of human behaviour, relationships, resources and institutions in local as well as global contexts, all of which are fundamental to our conception of society.

Cascade and the NEP

Based on an interactive pedagogy, the books focus on:

- Conceptual development encouraging students to learn how to learn through Constructivist learning tasks
- Thinking critically, solving problems and learning essential life skills to imbibe 21st century learning
- Creative skills aimed at developing all capabilities of learners and to increase individual happiness from childhood
- Multidisciplinary teaching which aligns to the NIPUN initiative for young learners
- Inquiring, analyzing and absorbing new information in a world of increasing interconnections through inferential and experiential tasks
- Sustainable Development Goals that hold the key to the future of mankind sensitizing young learners through a gradual study that builds environmental and social awareness
- The promotion of Indian arts and culture to inculcate a sense of identity as well as an appreciation of other cultures and identities
- Competency-based Structured Assessments For Analyzing Learning (SAFAL)

About the series editor

Padmini Sriraman, has worked in the field of education for more than four decades. She was the former Principal of The Hindu Senior Secondary School in Chennai. A recipient of the CBSE National Award, Padmini is an author, consultant, mentor, master trainer CBSE and resource person of COE CBSE Chennai. She has conducted many workshops and seminars for teachers and principals across India and abroad.

Key Features

Cascade offers features that focus on essential skills to assist learners achieve holistic learning through a multidisciplinary approach. In so doing, the series is aligned with the guidelines given in the National Education Policy, 2020.

Learning

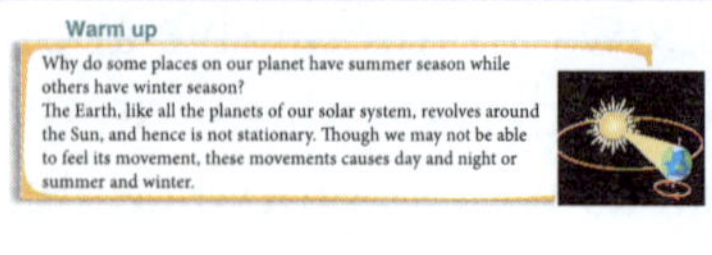

Warm up has pre-reading tasks for discovery-based learning

Conceptual Development

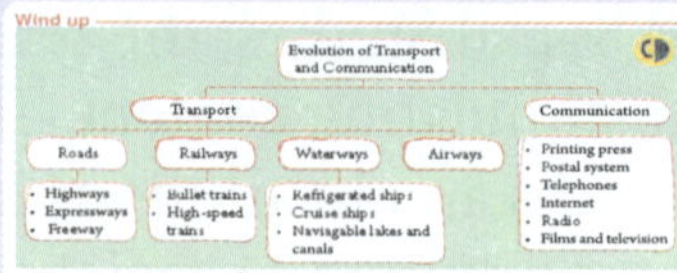

Wind Up has concept maps to assist in learning

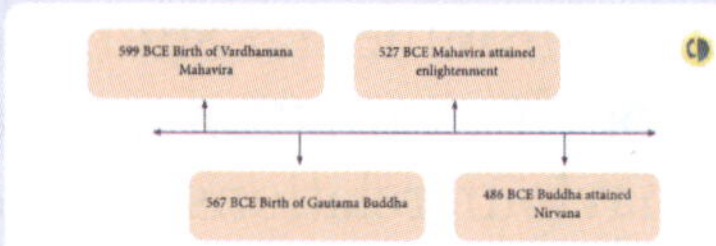

Timeline helps learners understand the chronology of events

Extended learning

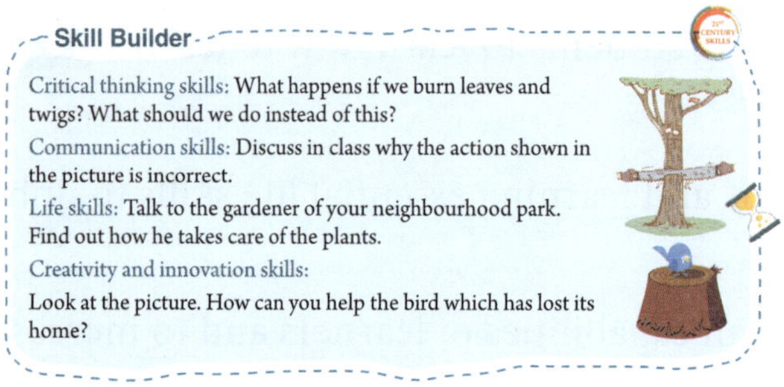

Skill builder has 21st century skills necessary in the age of information

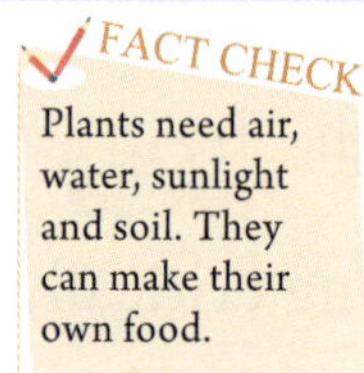

Fact check provides interesting titbits of information

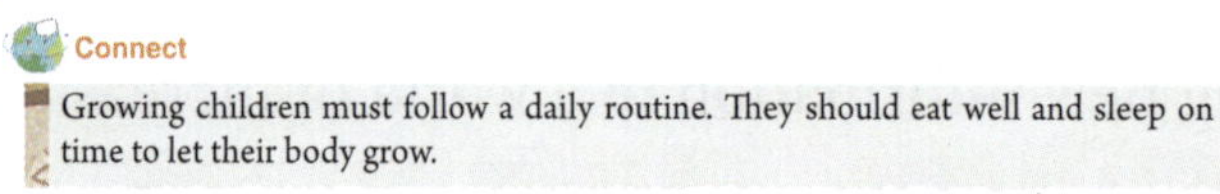

Connect highlights stories and events from around the world related to the chapter.

Green Earth sensitizes learners towards conservation of the environment.

Constructivist learning

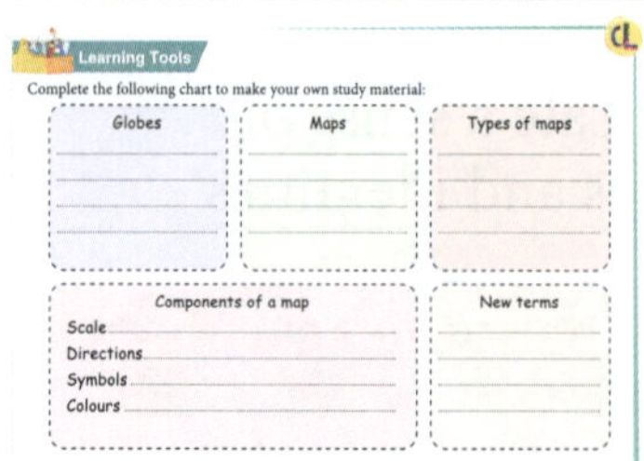

Learning Tools are student-made study guides to organize and arrange data encouraging self learning

Creativity and happiness

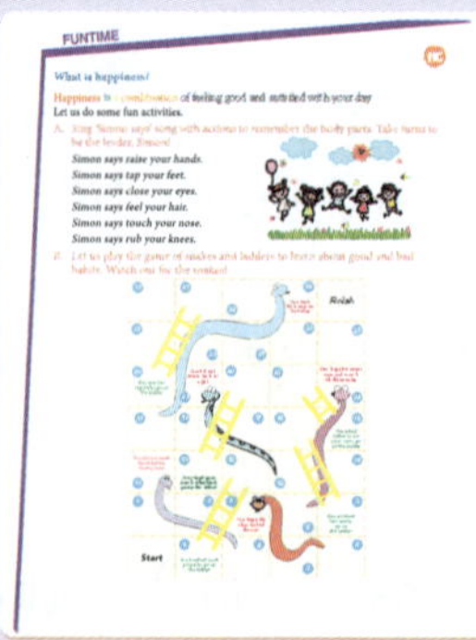

Fun Time addresses wellbeing and happiness of the students through creative and fun tasks

SDG Posters encourage sustainable living

Cross-curricular learning

What's in the picture?

Look at the family picnic picture. Name the sense organ that is being used by each person.

Mother:..................

Girl with dog:..................

Father:..................

Boy:..................

Girl:..................

What's in the picture? provides exercises for inferential learning

SAFAL

Geography skills

Use an atlas to find out the climatic zones in which the following countries are located:

1. India
2. United Kingdom
3. Finland
4. Kenya
5. South Africa
6. New Zealand

SAFAL

Geography skills build map skills and improve world overview of learners

Think Big

Data Fun

Hailey asked her friends about their favourite colour. She showed their answers by drawing circles in a table.

FAVORITE COLORS

Colour	Number of likes
Red	●●●
Blue	●●●●●
Yellow	●
Green	●●●
Purple	●●●●

How many of Hailey's friends chose blue as their favorite color?

Find out the favourite colour of 10-15 students in your class from the given choices. Draw coloured stars to show their answers in the table.

Colour	Number of students
Pink	✱
Orange	
Brown	
Yellow	
Green	

Say, how many of your friends chose green as their favourite colour.

Think Big provides varied activities for multidisciplinary learning

Observation and application

Apply it!

Look at the pictures. Write how the child is feeling.

....

Apply it! provides application-based activities for experiential learning

The Sahus

The Sahus have three children, Ajay, Sara and baby Raju. Mr. Sahu is a mason. He works hard to earn money and take care of his family. Ajay goes to school. But Sara needs to be at home to help her mother and to look after baby Raju. In the evening Ajay goes out to play with his friends but Sara does not as her mother asks her to look after her younger baby brother while she cooks for the family.

- Who all are there in the Sahu family?
- Do you think the children are treated equally? Discuss.
- Should Sara go to school?

Case Study re-counts in-depth investigations of a single person, group, event or community.

SAFAL

Assessment and practice

Exercises

A. Choose the correct answer to fill in the blanks.

1. .... is at the centre of the solar system.
   a. Mars b. Sun c. Earth
2. .... is the fifth planet from Earth.
   a. Mercury b. Jupiter c. Neptune

ASSESSMENT 1

A. Choose the correct option to fill in the blanks.

1. We live with our ____________
   a. friends b. family c. neighbours
2. We use our hands to ____________
   a. write b. kick c. run
3. We must wear a mask while going out as it ____________
   a. protects from pollution b. is fashion c. protects from illness
4. Our classrooms should be ____________
   a. dusty b. clean c. dark
5. A ____________ looks after us when we are sick.
   a. cleaner b. maid c. nurse

B. Write T for true and F for false sentences.

1. An identity card tells us nothing about the person wearing it.
2. Exercise keeps us fit for the whole day.
3. We must share work with our family members.
4. We can throw papers in the classroom.
5. Houses can be kutcha or pucca.

SAFAL

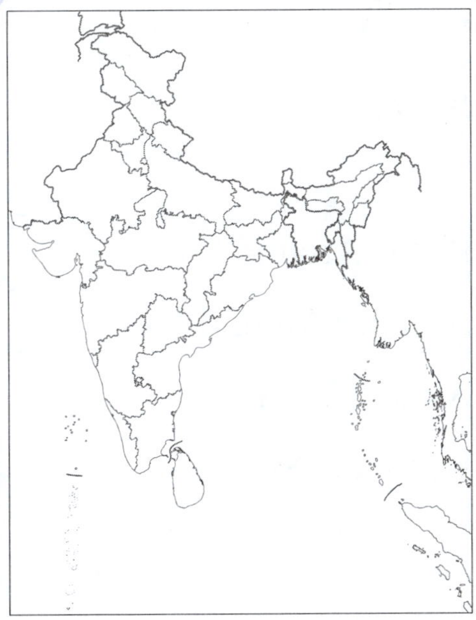

Exercises, **Assessments** and **Outline Maps** for assessment

CONTENTS

1. Meet Me

Warm up

Fill in the blanks to introduce yourself.

- My name is ____________.
- I am ____________ years old.
- My favourite colour is ____________.

Now draw your favourite toy.

Hello, I am Venkat. I am a boy. I am five years old. Bojo is my dog. I like to play with him every day.

Playing with my dog

I have many friends at school. Their names are Ina, Ishan and Jaskirat. We call Jaskirat, Jassi. It is her **nickname**.

Do you have a nickname too? Do you like people calling you by your nickname?

FACT CHECK

A friend is someone who knows you very well and likes you but who is not related to you.

Playing with my friends

My friends and I study together. We enjoy playing games. We must be kind to our friends. We must help one another and share our things too.

nickname: pet name of people

Identity Card

Have you seen children wearing cards in school?
These cards are called identity cards. The card tells us a few things about the person wearing it, such as their name, class and birthday.

Apply it! E

Complete the identity card.

School Name: ....

SCHOOL IDENTITY CARD

Paste photograph here

Class: .... Roll No.: ....

Name: ....

Date of Birth: ....

Green Earth

Trees are cut down to make paper. Use blank pages from old notebooks to draw to save paper.

Who else carries an identity card? Name at least two people.

Things We Like

The things that we enjoy the most are our **favourite** things. I like to draw, read, cycle and play with my toys. My friend likes to watch television. I like to sing in my free time. It is my **hobby**. Do you like to do any of the following activities? Circle your favourite one.

My drawing

Playing with toys

Dancing

Singing

favourite: something liked more than others of the same kind; hobby: something one likes to do in their free time

What's in the picture?

Join the numbers to complete the picture and colour it.

Skill Builder

Critical thinking skills: Venkat greets everyone by saying 'hello!' Think of three other words that you can use to greet people.

Life skills: We must be kind to our friends. Do you share your books with your friends?

Communicative skills: What makes you happy or sad? Write H for happy and S for sad.

- Having a toothache ....
- Getting wet in the rain ....
- Being hugged ....
- Eating a chocolate ....

Connect

Always share your things with your friends and do not trouble them.

Wind up

- Friends study and play together and help each other.
- The things we enjoy doing the most are our favourite things.
- A hobby is something we like to do in our free time.

Exercises

A. Choose the correct option to fill in the blanks.

1. Friends play ....

   a. together   b. alone

2. A pet name .... a nickname.
   a. is　　　　b. is not
3. The .... card tells us the name, class and age of the person.
   a. invitation　　　　b. identity
4. The things that we enjoy the .... are our favourite things.
   a. least　　　　b. most

B. Choose the correct words to complete the sentences.

hobby	enjoy	kind

1. We must be .... to our friends.
2. A .... is something that we like to do in our free time.
3. I .... with my friends.

C. Write Yes or No.

1. I wear glasses. ....
2. I have a nickname. ....
3. I have a hobby. ....
4. I have curly hair. ....

Think Big

Data Fun

Hailey asked her friends about their favourite colour. She showed their answers by drawing circles in a table.

FAVOURITE COLOURS	
Colour	Number of likes
Red	● ● ●
Blue	● ● ● ● ●
Yellow	●
Green	● ● ●
Purple	● ● ● ●

How many of Hailey's friends chose blue as their favourite colour?

Find out the favourite colour of 10-15 students in your class from the given choices. Draw coloured stars to show their answers in the table.

Colour	Number of students
Pink	★
Orange	
Brown	
Yellow	
Green	

Say, how many of your friends chose green as their favourite colour.

Learning Tools

Help Venkat and his friends reach their ice cream! Trace the lines with coloured pencil.

Web links:

https://www.bbc.co.uk/learningenglish/english/features/childrens-stories

https://www.education.com/activity/article/things-i-like-about-me/

Last accessed on 30 August 2021

2. Our Body

Warm up

Which part of your body helps you see things?

Our body helps us do various activities. It has many parts. Each part of our body is **important**. Let us learn about our body.

Parts of Our Body

Each part of our body performs a particular **function**. We use different parts of our body to carry out different actions. We breathe through our nose. We walk and jump using our legs. We hold things with our hands.

Look at the picture and read aloud the names of the body parts with your teacher.

Parts of the body

important: of great value; function: work or action

Sense Organs

We can see, hear, taste, smell and feel. Our eyes, ears, tongue, nose and skin help us do these things. These are called **sense organs**.

What's in the picture?

Eating

Reading

Playing ball

Look at the pictures and name the body parts that are being used to do these actions.

Apply it!

HC E

Sing along with your friends with actions.

I can see a bird wink and wink.
I can hear her song tweet and tweet.
And the fruits on trees smell so nice and taste so sweet.
I clap my hands, clap and clap.
And raise my legs, flip and flop.

1. What did you do in this song?
2. How many body parts do we have in pairs?

Green Earth

Sunshine helps our body become strong.

We see with our eyes.

We hear with our ears.

We taste with our tongue.

We smell with our nose.

We feel with our skin.

FACT CHECK

Our eyes close on their own to protect themselves when we look at the Sun directly or when there is dust around.

sense organs: parts of the body that help us see, hear, taste, smell and touch

Skill Builder

Critical thinking skills: Observe a bird, a dog, a cat and an ant. Think and say which part of the body these animals use to move.

Life skills: Find out which sense organs are these monkeys showing. What are they trying to say?

Connect

Remember that a healthy body is a valuable gift. We should look after it.

Wind up

- Our body helps us do many things.
- Each part of our body is useful.
- Our body has five sense organs.

Exercises

A. Circle the names of sense organs with red colour and other body parts with green colour.

eyes	legs	chin	tongue	head
ears	hands	skin	nose	lips

B. Write which body part or parts would you use to do these actions.

1. 

....

2. 

....

3. 

....

4. 

....

C. Match the sense organs with their corresponding action.

Column A		Column B	
1.		a.	
2.		b.	
3.		c.	
4.		d.	
5.		e.	

Think Big

Craft Fun

Make a handprint painting!

Material required: a sheet of paper, watercolours, pencil and crayons

Method:

1. Ask an adult to draw the body of a butterfly on a sheet.
2. Colour the butterfly's body.
3. Dip your palms in different colours and press them on either side of the insect's body.
4. Place them facing away from each other in different colours, as shown here.
5. Let the paint dry. Your butterfly would be ready to display.

Learning Tools

Read the sentences with picture clues. Tick (✓) the correct ones. One has been done for you.

1.

2.
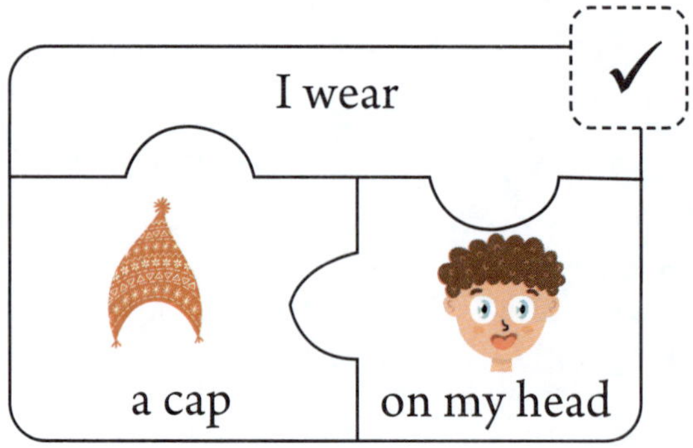

3.
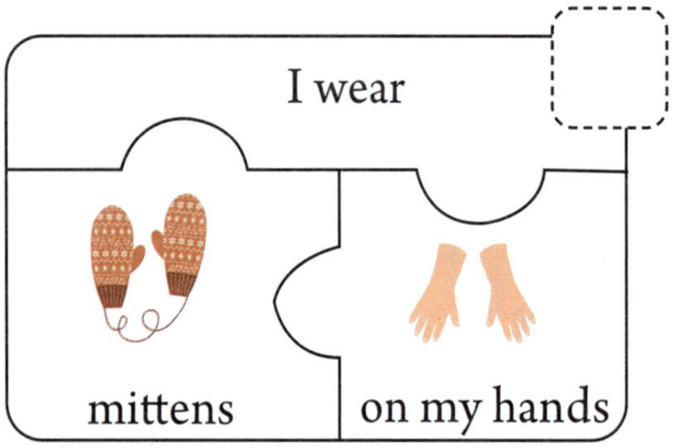

4.
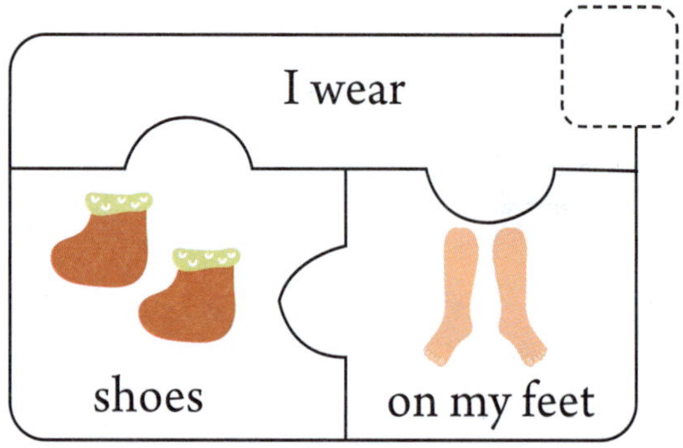

5.

6.
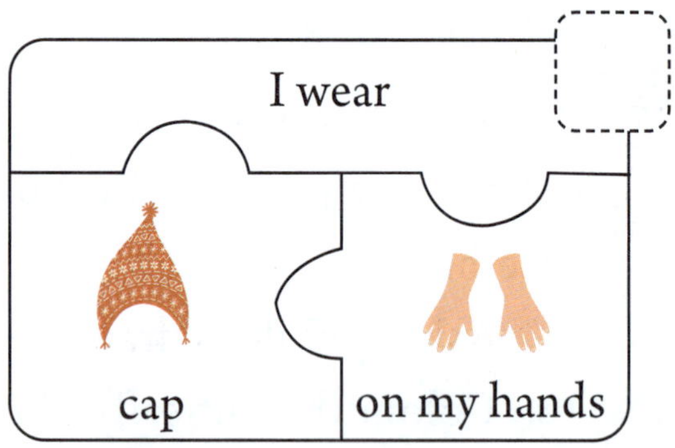

Web links:

https://learnenglishkids.britishcouncil.org/search/apachesolr_search/our%2520body
https://www.dkfindout.com/uk/

Last accessed on 30 August 2021

3. Healthy and Clean

Warm up

We have to keep our body healthy and clean.
How many times in a day do you take a bath?

We should take care of our body as it helps us do different activities. We should keep our body **healthy** and clean. This **prevents** us from falling sick.

Be Healthy

Doing something daily or often forms a habit. We should have healthy habits.

Exercise regularly

- Eat food that gives **energy** and keeps our body fit.
- Drink clean water always.
- **Exercise** regularly to stay fit and healthy.
- Sleep on time and wake up early.
- Breathe in fresh air.

FACT CHECK

Fingernails grow faster than toenails.

Stay Clean

Keeping our body clean keeps us healthy.

healthy: fit, in a good condition; prevents: stops something from happening; energy: strength to work; exercise: activity done to stay healthy

We should do the following activities to keep ourselves clean.

Take a bath daily.

Brush our teeth twice daily.

Trim our nails regularly.

Comb our hair neatly.

Wash our hands before and after eating food.

Green Earth

Be mindful of using water while doing your daily activities.

Apply it!

Tick (✓) the things that help us take care of our body.

 ☐

 ☐

 ☐

☐

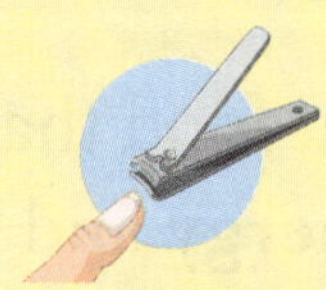 ☐

 ☐

We must keep our body safe and not play with sharp objects.

Be Safe

Do you know what makes us sick? Germs are tiny things that we cannot see. They can get inside our body through our hands, feet, nose or mouth. These germs make us sick. We must not let germs enter our body. To be safe, we must:

- Use hand sanitizer
- Eat food that gives us energy

Use hand sanitizer

- Stay away from crowded areas and maintain social distance
- Wear a mask while stepping out of home
- Drink clean water

Wear a mask outside

Maintain social distance

What's in the picture?

* SDG goal number 3 focus on good health and wellbeing. Look at pictures and tick (✓) the actions that would keep you healthy.

Skill Builder

Critical thinking skills:

A. Tia said, 'It is important to play and exercise daily'. Why is Tia right?

B. Which is the correct behaviour? Tick (✓) in the box.

1. We should eat junk food every day.
2. We should wash our hands before and after eating.
3. We should always eat breakfast.
4. We should keep long nails.

Life skills: You woke up late. It is time to go to school. What would you do? Tick (✓) the correct answer.

1. Skip brushing teeth
2. Eat breakfast slowly
3. Skip your exercise
4. Have a quick bath

Information literacy: Find out why we should clean our tongue while brushing teeth.

Connect

Playing outdoors is good for health. If playing outside is not possible, then do some light exercise at home.

* The Sustainable Development Goals (SDGs) are 17 global goals adopted by the United Nations in 2015. This is a universal call to all nations for action to end inequality, poverty, protect the planet and ensure that by 2030 all people enjoy peace and prosperity.

Wind up

- We should take care of our body.
- Keeping our body clean keeps us in good health.
- We should eat food that gives us energy and drink clean water.
- We should exercise regularly.
- We should keep our body safe.

Exercises

A. Write T for true and F for false.

1. It is not important to bathe daily. ☐
2. We should trim our nails regularly. ☐
3. We should brush our teeth twice a week. ☐
4. We should comb our hair neatly. ☐

B. Choose the correct word from the box to fill in the blanks.

exercise	sleep	clean	Germs	energy

1. We must keep our body ....
2. We should .... on time to give rest to our body.
3. We should .... daily to stay fit.
4. We should eat food that gives us ....
5. .... make us sick.

C. Answer the questions.

1. Why should we exercise every day?
2. What should we do when we get tired?
3. Write three ways in which we can keep our body safe.

Think Big

Art integration

Let's make a painting to show germs using straws.

Material required: watercolours, straws, sheets of paper, black marker and paints

Method:

1. Make a small puddle of paint on a sheet of paper with the paintbrush.
2. Blow on the paint with a straw towards left and right.

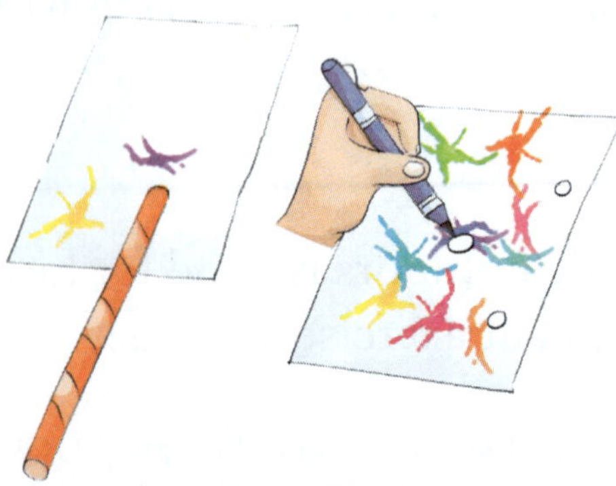

3. Let the paint dry. Draw two black circles in the centre and dots for the eyes.
4. Draw more lines from the centre to make the germs.

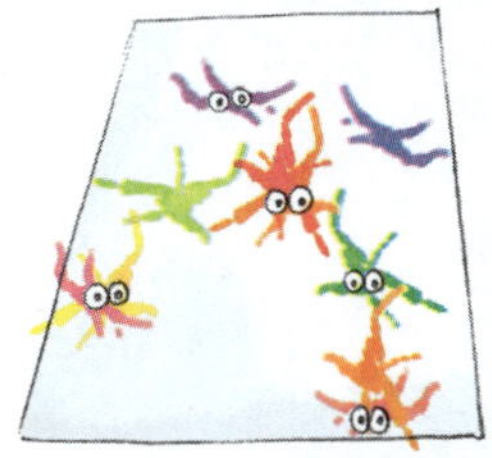

Learning Tools

Look at Zack's daily routine. Number them as per sequence. Colour the box green for the healthy habits which you also follow.

Web links:

https://learnenglishkids.britishcouncil.org/category/topics/daily-routines
https://kids.nationalgeographic.com/books/article/yoga-animals
Last accessed on 30 August 2021

4. Our Family

Warm up

Name any two of your family members.

______________________ ______________________

A family is a group of people living together. Parents and their children are members of a family.

Our parents are our mother and father. Their parents are our grandparents. Our sisters and brothers are called our siblings. A pet is also a part of the family.

Types of Families

A family can be big or small. Parents and children living together make a small family.

Parents, grandparents and children living together make a large family. Sometimes, an **uncle**, an **aunt** and their children also live with them. This family is called a joint family. Children of your uncle or aunt are called your cousins.

A small family

A joint family

uncle: the brother of your mother or father or the husband of your aunt; aunt: the sister of your mother or father or the wife of your uncle

What's in the picture?

Circle the family members who live with you.

FACT CHECK

A family that consists of only one parent and his or her children living together is called a one-parent family.

Fun with Family

All members of a family have fun together. They eat together and laugh and play together.

They enjoy at home by playing games and watching television. They **celebrate festivals** together. They go out for picnics, visit people and other places.

Family members love and care for each other. We must respect our elders at home and listen to their advice. We must help our parents in keeping the house clean and tidy.

Green Earth

Ask your family members to use cloth or paper bags in place of plastic bags.

Playing together

Celebrating together

Going out together

Apply it!

E

How do you have fun with your family? Tick (✓) the correct options.

- Go to school ☐
- Do homework ☐
- Celebrate festivals ☐
- Go for picnic ☐
- Visit malls ☐
- Eat dinner together ☐

celebrate: to enjoy a special day; festival: a time or day of feasting or celebration

Skill Builder

Critical thinking skills: Do you know your family? Name these people.

1. The most caring member ....
2. The best cook ....
3. The tallest member ....
4. The most fun-loving member ....

Information literacy: Do animals have families? Can you name the young ones of lions, cats and dogs?

Life skills: Write your parents' mobile numbers.

1. Mother's number .... 2. Father's number ....

Connect

The largest joint family in the world with 193 members is from Mizoram, India.

Wind up

- A family is a group of people living together.
- A family can be small or large.
- Family members love and care for each other.

Exercises

A. Choose the correct option to fill in the blanks.

1. The members of a family live ....
   a. together b. separately
2. A .... is also a part of the family.
   a. stranger b. pet
3. The members of a family have .... together.
   a. fight b. fun
4. A family can be small or ....
   a. big b. little
5. Children of your uncle or aunt are your ....
   a. friends b. cousins

B. Who does these activities for you in your family?

1. Buys you things ....
2. Gets you ready for school ....
3. Cleans the house ....
4. Helps you with homework ....

C. Match the columns.

	Column A		Column B
1.	Small family	a.	Father's or mother's sister
2.	Uncle	b.	Mother's or father's parents
3.	Grandparents	c.	Parents and children
4.	Aunt	d.	Mother's or father's brother

Think Big

Craft Fun

Make a 'My Family' poster.

Take five or six ice cream sticks. Draw the faces of your family members on these sticks. Paste the sticks on a sheet and pin it up. Write one line about each of them and present it to the class.

Learning Tools

Let's play Family Bingo!! Circle the words you would connect with family.

Lullaby	Visiting grandma	Wedding	Kitten	Eating out
Grandfather	Car	Sun	Vacation	Orange
Cousin	Tree	Festival	Picnic	Class

Web links:

https://www.natgeokids.com/uk/?s=family&post_type=primary-resource

Last accessed on 30 Aug 2021

Worksheet (Chapters 1-4)

A. Match the organs with the actions.

	Column A		Column B
1.	Nose	a.	Running
2.	Ears	b.	Drawing
3.	Legs	c.	Listening to music
4.	Hands	d.	Watching TV
5.	Eyes	e.	Smelling

B. Colour the boxes green for the activities that you should do to stay healthy.

 ☐

 ☐

 ☐

 ☐

 ☐

 ☐

C. Choose the correct option to fill in the blanks.

1. The .... card tells our name, class and birthday.
   a. identity   b. birthday   c. gift
2. The things that we enjoy doing the most in our free time is called our ....
   a. habit   b. hobby   c. duty
3. A .... is a group of people living together.
   a. friends   b. siblings   c. family
4. Our sisters and brothers are called our ....
   a. siblings   b. friends   c. teachers
5. Parents and children living together make a .... family.
   a. joint   b. small   c. large

5. School is Fun

Warm up

Circle the activities that you do in school.

At School

I learn to read, write and count in school. I also learn to draw, play and sing. I wear a uniform when I go to school. I go to school in the school bus. My friend comes to school on her bicycle.

What's in the picture?

How are the students coming to the school? Tick (✓) the correct boxes.

- Walk ☐
- Cycle ☐
- By car ☐
- By bus ☐

I have many friends in school.
I play and share things with them.

I study in a classroom.
A classroom has many desks and chairs, display boards and a blackboard.

In a classroom

Places in School

A school has different places to do various activities.

I play in the school playground.

I go to the library to read and **borrow** books.

I go to the computer lab to learn about computers.

I go to the music room to learn music.

I eat lunch in the school canteen.

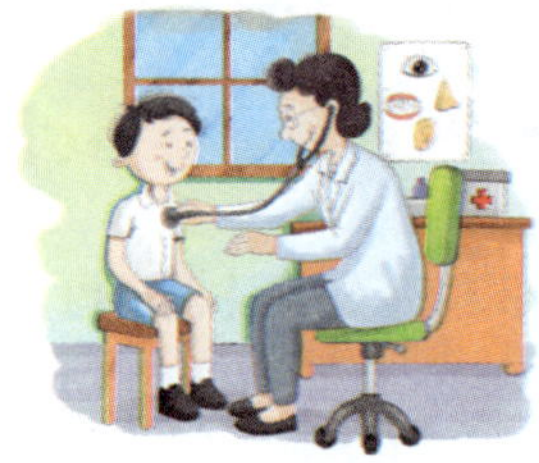

I go to the medical room if I get hurt.

The head of a school is the Principal, who has his/her own office in the school. School functions are held in the auditorium.

Apply it!

Tick (✓) the things you take to school.

☐ ☐ ☐ ☐ ☐ ☐ ☐ ☐

Respect for School

I greet our teachers every day and learn to be **polite**.
I take care of my school and keep it clean.

FACT CHECK

A boarding school is a place where students live and study.

borrow: to take and use something that belongs to someone else and return it later; polite: to speak softly with respect

We must respect our school by taking care of the places and the things that we use in the school.

Keep classroom clean

Green Earth

Keep a plant near a window in your class and take turns to water it.

Skill Builder

21ST CENTURY SKILLS

Critical thinking skills: How do you go to school? Is this mode of transport good for the environment?

Communicative skills: Talk about your favourite class in school.

Life skills: If you were sitting in the last row and were unable to see the blackboard, what would you do?

Connect

Remember to switch off the lights and fans in the classroom when you leave.

Wind up

- In school, we learn to read, write, count, draw, sing and work together.
- There are different places in a school to do various activities.
- We should keep our school clean.

Exercises

A. Colour the box green for the activities you do in school.

1. Count	☐	2. Sleep	☐
3. Read	☐	4. Draw	☐
5. Watch TV	☐	6. Write	☐

B. Choose the correct word from the box and name the pictures.

classroom	library	playground	music room

....

C. Choose the correct options to fill in the blanks.

read	play	uniform	learn

1. I wear a .... to school.
2. I .... about computers in the computer lab.
3. I .... with my friends in the playground.
4. I .... in the library.

Think Big — Number Fun

There are more than eight pencils hidden in the picture below. Find them and circle!

Learning Tools

1. Meena has to get ready for school. What should she do first? Number the given pictures in sequence.

2. Draw a happy face or a sad face for these actions in school.
    1. Greet your friends and teacher
    2. Not share your colours with anyone
    3. Wait for your turn in the playground
    4. Switch off the fans after class
    5. Listen to your teacher
    6. Climb on your chair in class

Web links:

https://www.natgeokids.com/uk/kids-club/entertainment/general-entertainment/masha-bear-school-quiz/

Last accessed on 30 August 2021

Respect for School

We must respect our school by taking care of the places and the things we use in the school. We should also respect the people in our school. We must take care of our classmates.

We should not write on the library books or tear their pages.

We should put things back after using them.

We should throw trash in the dustbin.

We should not **scribble** on walls, desks and chairs in the classroom.

We should not pluck flowers or break the plants growing in the school.

We should wait for our turn while playing in the playground.

We should clean the blackboard and **arrange** the chairs in our classroom to keep it clean.

We should decorate our classroom.

We should respect our teachers.

scribble: to write something quickly; arrange: to plan or organise something

6. Places Around Us

Warm up

Look at the pictures. Where would you see these people?

__________ __________ __________

The people who live near our house are our neighbours. The area around our house is our neighbourhood. There are many places in a neighbourhood, like a park, a school, a hospital, a post office and a market.

Park

Places in a Neighbourhood

We play in our neighbourhood **park**. Playing in the park helps us stay fit and healthy.

When we fall sick, we visit a doctor in a clinic or a hospital in the neighbourhood.

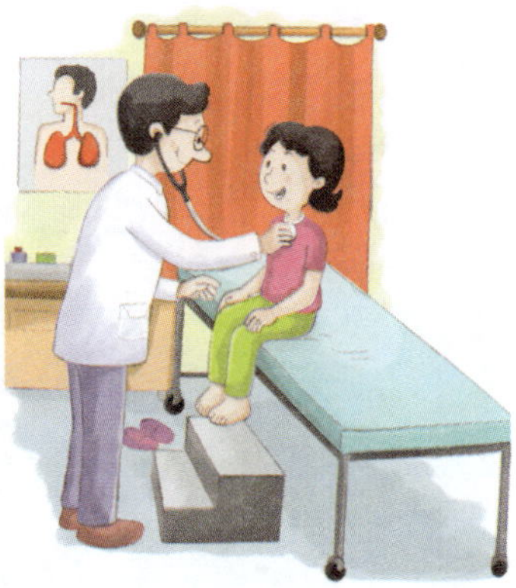

Clinic

A post office is from where we send letters and cards to our family and friends who live far away.

Post Office

park: a place where people play, walk and relax

A police station is an important part of our neighbourhood. Police officers protect us from thieves.

Sometimes, there is a school in the neighbourhood. Many neighbourhoods also have bus stops from where we can board a bus.

Police Station

> **FACT CHECK**
>
> India has the largest number of post offices in the world.

A neighbourhood also has a market with many shops. We buy fruits and vegetables from a **greengrocer**.

We go to a restaurant to eat. We keep our money safe in a bank.

School

Apply it!

Where would these people go to get their work done? Name the places.

1. Gurpreet should buy apples from a ....
2. Uncle Sunil wants to keep his money safe. He should go to a ....
3. Mrs Rai is feeling sick. She should go to a ....

A Good Neighbourhood

A good neighbourhood has all the places that we need. We should keep our neighbourhood clean. We should be kind and helpful to our neighbours.

> **Green Earth**
>
> Always eat properly and do not waste food in a restaurant.

What's in the picture?

Look at the picture and name any four places that you can see.

....

....

greengrocer: a person who sells fruits and vegetables

Skill Builder

21ST CENTURY SKILLS

Critical thinking skills: Think of any three ways in which you can help your neighbours.

Life skills: Your neighbour has asked you to help him fill some bottles of water from your house. Choose what would you do.

1. Watch TV and not fill the bottles. ☐
2. Fill the bottles and ask your sibling to help you. ☐
3. Ask your helper to do it. ☐

Connect

Stay away from strangers in the neighbourhood.

Wind up

- People who live near our house are our neighbours.
- The area around our house is called our neighbourhood.
- We have different places in a neighbourhood.

Exercises

A. Choose the correct option to fill in the blanks.

1. A .... is the area around our house.

   a. park b. neighbourhood c. shop

2. People who live in the same neighbourhood are called ....

   a. friends b. family c. neighbours

3. We go to a .... to play and walk.

   a. market b. park c. post office

4. We go to a .... when we fall sick.

   a. hospital b. bank c. market

B. Match the following.

police station   bus stop   restaurant   hospital

C. Write T for true and F for false.

1. Police officer protects us from thieves. ☐
2. We buy fruits from a post office. ☐
3. We go to a park when we fall sick. ☐
4. We go to a market to buy things. ☐
5. We should not help our neighbours. ☐

Think Big

Number fun

Look at the neighbourhood park. Count and write the number of things you can see in the park.

- Swings ....
- Slides ....
- See saw ....
- Jungle gym ....
- Sand pit ....
- Trees ....
- Benches ....

Learning Tools

A. Write one sentence for each of the given places.

Market	Hospital	Police station
....	....	....
....	....	....

Restaurant	Post office	Bank
....	....	....
....	....	....

B. Trace the path to help Mili reach her home.

Web links:

https://kids.nationalgeographic.com/nature/article/clean-it-up

Last accessed on 30 August 2021

7. Helping Hands

Warm up

Who washes your clothes at home? What do you think would happen if that person does not come for a few days?

Our Helpers

There are many people who help us in our daily lives. They help us with the things that we cannot do ourselves. They help us at home, in school and in our neighbourhood. They are our community helpers.

Green Earth

Plants and trees keep the air clean. A gardener takes care of plants and trees.

A teacher teaches us to read and write.

A doctor treats us when we are sick.

A tailor stitches our clothes.

A greengrocer sells fresh fruits and vegetables.

A traffic police officer controls traffic.

A carpenter makes wooden tables and chairs.

A bus driver takes us to school and brings us back home.

A shopkeeper sells goods we use daily.

A farmer grows crops for us.

A postman brings letters to our homes.

A cleaner sweeps the street and surroundings to keep it clean.

A nurse looks after us when we are sick.

Apply it!

Read this rhyme and answer the questions.

Cobbler, Cobbler, what do you do?
I mend your shoes and polish
them too!

Gardener, Gardener, what do you do? I
help keep your garden green under the
sky so blue.

Barber, Barber, what do you do? I cut
your hair and style it too.

1. What does a cobbler use to polish our shoes?
2. What does the gardener use to keep our garden beautiful?
3. What does a barber use to cut our hair?

FACT CHECK

Some people help animals. A doctor who treats animals is called a veterinarian.

Community helpers help us live a **comfortable** life. We should be thankful to them and treat them with respect. Just as helpers help us, we too should try to help the people around us.

What's in the picture?

1. Can you identify this community helper?
2. Have you seen them in your neighbourhood?
3. How do they help us?

Skill Builder

21ST CENTURY SKILLS

Critical thinking skills: Imagine that the community helper who cleans your neighbourhood does not come for a week. What do you think will happen?

Collaborative skills: Is it possible for us to learn any one work done by the helpers? If so, what work do you think can be done by us?

Life skills:

A. Your gardener steps on a spade and cuts his foot while working. What would you do? Tick (✓) the correct options.

1. Run inside your house for help. ☐
2. Bring the first-aid kit. ☐
3. Stand there and watch. ☐

B. What are the emergency numbers to call the police and the fire station?

Connect

Always speak politely to your helpers and thank them for their work.

Wind up

- Many people help us at home, in school and in the neighbourhood.
- We should be thankful to our community helpers and treat them with respect.

comfortable: giving comfort, at ease

Exercises

A. Choose the correct option to fill in the blanks.

1. A .... makes chairs for us.
   a. gardener b. carpenter c. cobbler
2. A .... mends our shoes.
   a. cobbler b. pilot c. doctor
3. A .... grows crops for us.
   a. farmer b. baker c. shopkeeper
4. A .... teaches us how to read and write.
   a. nurse b. teacher c. gardener
5. A .... stitches our clothes.
   a. carpenter b. tailor c. barber

B. Match the people to the things they use.

Column A		Column B
1. Traffic police	a.	
2. Tailor	b.	
3. Doctor	c.	
4. Gardener	d.	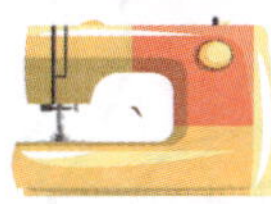

C. Unscramble the letters to get the name of the helper.

1. TAEHCRE .... 2. TSPMAON ....
3. BBCLREO .... 4. RFMRAE ....

Think Big — Craft Fun

Thank your helpers!

- Make a list of people who help you at home, like the house help, milkman, gardener, cook, guard and others.
- Take a chart paper and draw smiling faces on it.
- Colour them and cut them out. Take help of an adult.
- Give these to the helpers to thank them for their work.

Learning Tools

Trace the path to help the worker collect all his tools. You can also colour the picture.

Web links:

https://www.education.com/lesson-plan/community-helpers/
https://www.nationalgeographic.org/education/

Last accessed on 30 August 2021

8. Houses Around Us

Warm up

Have you seen a home of any bird? What is the home of a bird called?

We live with our family in a house. This house is called our home. Our home **protects** us from rain, wind, cold, heat, wild animals and thieves.

Types of Houses

There are many kinds of houses. Some are small and some are big. Houses that are made of mud, bamboo and straw are called kutcha houses. Houses made of bricks, cement and steel are called pucca houses.

Kutcha house

Pucca house

Places in a House

A house has different rooms for different activities.

It has bedrooms for sleeping, a kitchen for cooking food and a bathroom for bathing and washing.

It has a dining room for having breakfast, lunch and dinner with family.

Living room

It has a living room to sit with friends and **guests**.

protect: to protect someone or something means to prevent them from being harmed or damaged; guests: people who have been invited to your house

What's in the picture?

Label the rooms found in a house.

FACT CHECK

The early humans lived in natural caves or rock shelters.

Clean Home

We should keep our homes neat and clean. We should help our parents keep the house clean. We should keep our books and toys in their proper place. We should keep our shoes in the shoerack and throw waste in dustbins. A clean home keeps us healthy and happy.

Home should be clean and airy

Green Earth

We should keep plants near windows and in balconies as they make the air clean.

Apply it!

Talk to your grandparents and find out how did they keep their homes cool without any air conditioners.

Skill Builder

Critical thinking skills: Every household has a set of rules that need to be followed. Make a list of three rules you should follow to make your house safe and comfortable. Remember to follow them at home.

Life skills: Tick (✓) the things you would do to keep your home clean.

Connect

People keep windows open and let sunlight and fresh air enter the house.

Wind up

- A house protects us from rain, wind, cold, heat, wild animals and thieves.
- A house can be kutcha house or a pucca house.
- A house is called a home when we live with our family.
- A house has different rooms for different activities.
- We should keep our homes neat and clean.

Exercises

A. Choose the correct option to fill in the blanks.

1. A house is called a .... when we live with our family.

   a. hotel b. hostel c. home

2. The two kinds of houses are .... and ....

   a. brick and cement b. kutcha and pucca c. high and low

3. A .... is a room used for eating meals with the family.

   a. dining room b. bed room c. bath room

4. We should keep our homes .... and ....

   a. dusty and dirty b. neat and clean c. wet and cold

B. Match the columns.

	Column A		Column B
1.	Kitchen	a.	sitting with family and guests
2.	Bedroom	b.	bathing and washing
3.	Bathroom	c.	resting and sleeping
4.	Living room	d.	cooking food

C. Name the rooms where you can find these things.

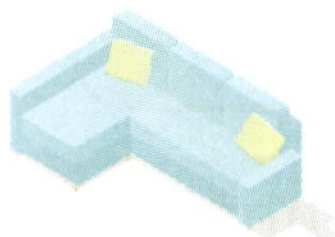    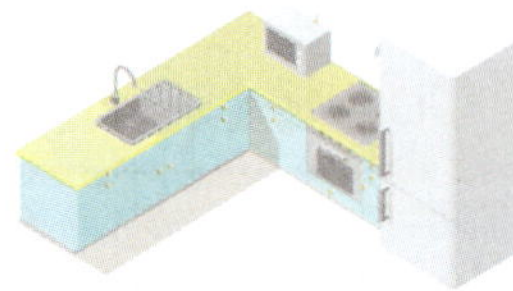

__________ __________ __________ __________ __________

Think Big — Colouring Fun

Join the dots and colour the house. You can create a garden too.

Learning Tools

Complete the following chart and tell us about your home.

Kutcha or pucca house?	Number of rooms	Does it have a balcony or garden?
....	....	....

Special feature	Your favourite room
....	....
....	....
	....

Web links:

https://www.nationalgeographic.org/education/

Last accessed on 30 August 2021

WORKSHEET

Worksheet (Chapters 5-8)

A. Look at the pictures and name them using the help box.

Tailor	Post Office	Library	Cleaner	Music Room	Park

1. 
....

2. 
....

3. 
....

4. 
....

5. 
....

6. 
....

B. Choose the correct option to fill in the blanks.

1. A .... mends our shoes.
   a. doctor b. nurse c. cobbler
2. School functions are held in the ....
   a. classroom b. auditorium c. computer lab
3. A doctor works in a ....
   a. hospital b. garden c. shop
4. We buy fruits and vegetables from a ....
   a. post office b. greengrocer c. bank
5. We sit with our friends and guests in our ....
   a. kitchen b. bedroom c. living room

C. Write T for true and F for false.

1. We should respect our teachers. ☐
2. Kutcha houses are made of cement and bricks. ☐
3. We should not keep our neighbourhood clean. ☐
4. A post office helps us send letters and cards. ☐
5. A carpenter fixes pipes and taps. ☐

9. Food and Clothes

Warm up

- Tick which food is healthier

☐ ☐

- What is the girl wearing to protect herself from the cold?

Food is important for all of us. We need food to live, grow and stay healthy. Food also gives us **energy** to work and play.

Food We Eat

We eat different kinds of food. They include fruits, vegetables, grains, meat and milk products.

We get fruits, vegetables and grains from plants. We get milk, meat and eggs from animals.

FACT CHECK

Water is just as important as food. We should drink six to eight glasses of water every day.

Apply it!

Match the food groups with their names.

1. 
2. 
3. 
4. 
5. 

a. Vegetables b. Milk products c. Meat d. Fruits e. Grains

energy: the ability and strength to do active physical activities

Meals We Have

In a day, we have three **meals**. We eat breakfast in the morning, lunch in the afternoon and dinner at night. Breakfast is the most important meal of the day. We also eat **snacks** between breakfast and lunch, and again between lunch and dinner.

Breakfast

Lunch

Dinner

Good Food Habits

Food eaten in the right amount is healthy food. We should eat healthy meals. We should always eat fresh and clean food. Some food items that are not healthy are called junk food. We should avoid eating junk food.

Always wash your hands before and after eating.

Eat fresh food and chew it well.

Do not waste food or throw it away.

Do not overeat.

FACT CHECK

Long ago, people used leaves or animal skin as clothes to protect themselves from cold.

Clothes

Clothes cover our body. They protect us from heat, cold and rain. They also keep us safe from insect bites, dust and dirt.

meal: food that we eat at a particular time; snacks: small amounts of food eaten between meals

Types of Clothes

Woollen clothes keep us warm

We wear different kinds of clothes in different seasons. We wear light, **cotton** clothes when it is hot. Cotton clothes keep our body cool.

When it is cold, we wear **woollen** clothes to keep our body warm. Woollen clothes are made of wool.

Raincoat keeps us dry in rain

When it rains, we wear raincoats, gumboots and carry umbrellas. Raincoats are made of rubber or plastic. Raincoats do get wet but do not let water **seep** into us and they dry quickly. We also wear rubber shoes called gumboots that are fit for the rainy season.

We wear uniforms to school

Sometimes a group of people wear special clothes. These are known as uniforms. We too wear uniforms to school.

Green Earth

The cotton plant gives fibre for cotton clothes and its seeds are used as food for animals.

What's in the picture?

....

....

....

....

Name these helpers who wear a special uniform.

cotton: clothes that are made from the cotton plant; woollen: clothes that are made from wool; seep: to leak through

Skill Builder

Critical thinking skills:

A. How do you react when you are hungry and find that the food made at home is not to your liking? Should you only eat the food items that you like?

B. Name any three things that a tailor would use to make a shirt for you.

Life skills:

A. You wake up late every morning and then rush to reach school. So, you miss having your breakfast each morning. What should you do?

1. Start waking up early. ☐
2. Keep waking up late. ☐
3. Eat breakfast anyway and reach your school late. ☐

B. Which clothes do we wear when we go for swimming?

Connect

Healthy food and clean clothes help us to be smart and fit.

Wind up

- Food gives us energy to live, grow, work and play.
- We have three meals in a day—breakfast, lunch and dinner.
- We should eat healthy meals.
- Clothes protect us from heat, cold, rain and insect bites.
- We wear different clothes in different seasons.
- We sometimes wear special clothes to work called uniform.

Exercises

A. Write T for true and F for false.

1. We should not eat food properly. ☐
2. Food keeps us healthy and gives us energy. ☐
3. Clothes protect us from dust and thieves. ☐
4. We wear different clothes in different seasons. ☐
5. We have lunch at night. ☐

B. Choose the correct option to fill in the blanks.

1. .... gives us energy to work and play.

   a. Medicine b. Food c. Clothes

2. We wear clothes to protect us from ....

   a. heat and cold b. eat and grow c. play and games

3. We eat some .... between breakfast and lunch, and between lunch and dinner.

   a. air b. snacks c. plastic

4. Silk and woollen clothes keep us ....

   a. warm b. dry c. cool

5. .... are worn to keep us dry during rains.

   a. Shorts and slippers b. Raincoat and gumboots c. uniform and skirt

C. Answer these questions.

1. Which type of food should we eat?
2. Name one food each that we get from plants and animals.
3. How do clothes help us?
4. What are clothes made of?

Think Big — Number Fun

Look at the pictures and solve the given equations. One has been done for you.

1.  4 – 1 = 3

2.  .... = ?

3.  .... = ?

4.  .... = ?

5.  .... = ?

6.  .... = ?

Learning Tools

A. Circle the food items that you like and say whether they are healthy or not.

B. Look at the pictures and find the words in the word search.

C	O	A	T	R	D	I	S	N	E
S	D	R	E	S	S	O	W	E	H
V	B	P	E	D	R	U	E	I	A
S	H	O	R	T	S	E	A	Y	T
O	J	E	A	N	S	T	T	R	U
L	U	N	T	E	R	F	E	Y	T
T	S	H	I	R	T	Y	R	T	E
N	F	L	Y	H	S	O	C	K	S
S	K	I	R	T	U	R	I	N	E
M	S	W	I	M	S	U	I	T	E

Web links:

https://www.dkfindout.com/uk/explore/why-should-we-eat-foods-different-colours/

https://www.education.com/resources/?q=clothes

Last accessed on 30 August 2021

10. Let Us Celebrate

Warm up

Which all festivals do you celebrate with your family? Discuss.

We celebrate special days with our family and friends. Birthdays, weddings and festivals are special days.

How do you celebrate your birthday with your family?

A festival is a special time that we celebrate every year with family and friends. We wear new clothes, eat special food and **exchange** gifts and sweets with each other.

Celebrating birthday

In India, we celebrate different festivals. Festivals bring joy and happiness to all.

Diwali

Diwali is known as the 'Festival of Lights'. On this day, people pray and make rangoli to **decorate** their homes. They light *diyas* and candles, make sweets and invite friends and relatives for a **feast**.

Celebrating Diwali

exchange: doing or giving something to someone in return for something else; decorate: to make something look good by putting nice things on it; feast: a special meal eaten together to celebrate special days

Green Earth

Bursting crackers makes the air dirty.

Christmas

Celebrating Christmas

Christmas is celebrated on 25th of December as the birthday of Jesus Christ. People go to church to pray and decorate their homes with a Christmas tree. They make cakes and exchange gifts with family and friends.

Gurpurab

Celebrating Gurpurab

On Gurpurab, people celebrate Guru Nanak's birthday. On this day, people pray in a gurdwara. They eat a community meal called langar.

Eid-ul-Fitr

Celebrating Eid

Eid-ul-Fitr is another festival celebrated in India. On this day, people go to a mosque to pray. A special sweet dish called *seviyan* is prepared. People have a **grand** feast with friends and relatives.

Apply it!

Match the places of worship to their names.

1. 
2. 
3. 
4. 

a. Temple b. Church c. Mosque d. Gurdwara

grand: large and important

National Festivals

Independence Day

All Indians celebrate three special days known as national festivals.

Independence Day is celebrated on 15th August every year as India became a free country on this day. Our flag is hoisted in a ceremony at Red Fort in Delhi.

> **FACT CHECK**
>
> The second president of India was Dr Sarvepalli Radhakrishnan. His birthday is celebrated as Teacher's Day on 5th September each year.

Republic Day is celebrated on 26th January each year. A parade is held at Rajpath on this day.

Gandhi Jayanti is celebrated on 2nd October every year. On this day, Mahatma Gandhi was born.

Republic Day

Gandhi Jayanti

What's in the picture?

Look at the pictures and identify the festivals related to it.

....

....

....

Skill Builder

Critical thinking skills: Why do dogs run away when people burst crackers during festivals?

Life skills: Your neighbours have invited your family to celebrate their festival with them. What would you do?

1. Share their celebrations
2. Understand and appreciate their festival
3. Make an excuse and not go to your neighbour's house

Connect

Festivals celebrated with feasts, lights, dance and fun help people in all countries, connect with their families and friends.

Wind up

- A festival is a special time that we celebrate every year with family and friends.
- Diwali, Eid, Christmas and Gurpurab are some of the festivals that we celebrate.
- Independence Day, Republic Day and Gandhi Jayanti are national festivals.

Exercises

A. Match the pictures to their names.

Column A	Column B
1. 	a. Christmas
2. 	b. Republic Day
3. 	c. Diwali
4. 	d. Gurpurab

B. Choose the correct option to fill in the blanks.

1. A festival is a special time which we celebrate with our ....
   a. family   b. doctors   c. helpers
2. During Christmas, people go to the ....
   a. temple   b. church   c. gurdwara
3. India became a free country on the..............................
   a. Republic Day   b. Independence Day   c. New Year Day
4. On 5th September, we celebrate the birthday of ....
   a. Jawaharlal Nehru   b. S. Radhakrishnan   c. Mahatma Gandhi
5. Guru Nanak's birthday is called ....
   a. Diwali   b. Eid-ul-Fitr   c. Gurpurab

C. Name the following.

1. The community feast held on Gurpurab ....
2. A festival which is also known as the Festival of Lights ....
3. A special dish prepared during Eid ....
4. Independence Day is this festival ....
5. A festival celebrated on 2nd October every year ....

Think Big

Number Fun

Complete the maze and help the animals reach their cakes! Write down their age in the box given below.

- Giraffe ☐
- Rabbit ☐
- Monkey ☐
- Bear ☐

Learning Tools

1. Circle the words connected to a festival.

gifts	swing	family	lights
new clothes	bus	special dish	chalk
fun	cleaning	water	pillow

2. Complete colouring the christmas tree according to the given colours.

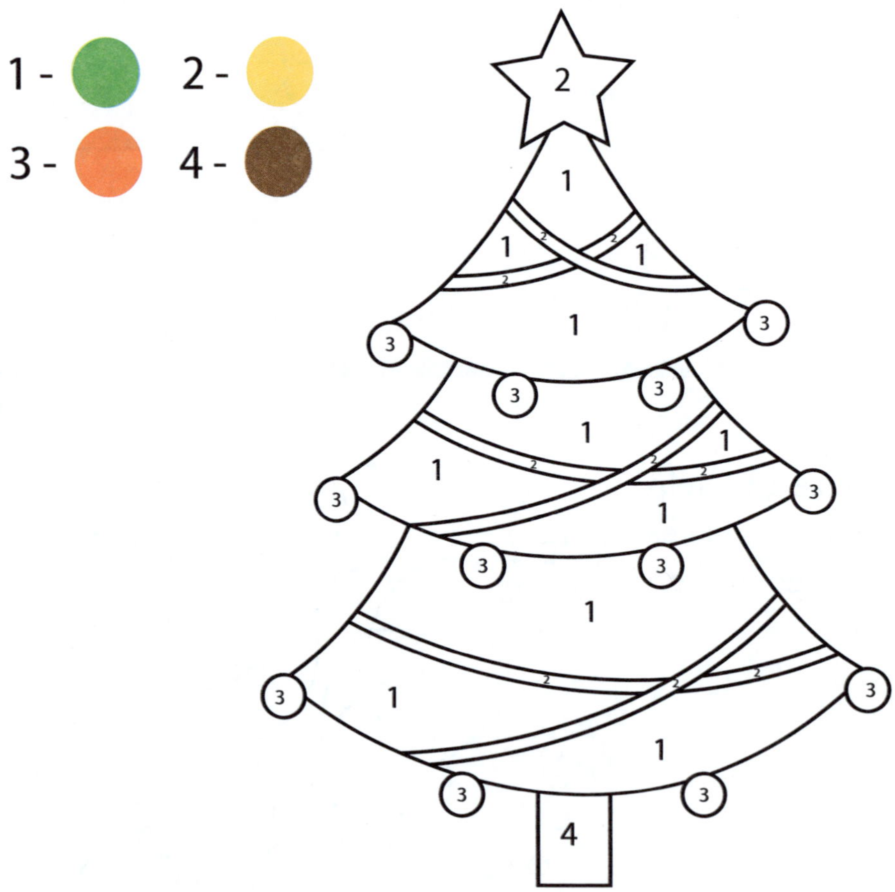

Web links:

https://www.india.gov.in/topics/art-culture/fairs-festivals
https://www.dkfindout.com/uk/search/festivals/
Last accessed on 30 August 2021

11. Ways We Travel

Warm up

Look at the traffic on a street in the picture.

1. Name the vehicles you see.
2. Which is your favorite vehicle?

We travel when we go from one place to another. Any **vehicle** that one can travel or carry goods in is a **means of transport**. The different means of transport take us from one place to another. We travel to the school, to work, to the market and for vacations.

Vehicles

We use different kinds of vehicles to travel. Most vehicles run on wheels, such as cars and buses. Vehicles that travel on water do not run on wheels.

Vehicles can be fast or slow. A rickshaw, a cycle and a bullock cart move slowly. A car, a bus, a train, a metro and an aeroplane move fast.

Fast and slow vehicles

vehicle: machine that take people from one place to another; means of transport: the different ways by which we travel such as land, air, water transport

What's in the picture?

Observe these vehicles and write the number of wheels each vehicle has.

Ways We Travel

Vehicles move on land, air or water. Vehicles such as cars, cycles, buses and trains travel on land. In some villages, bullock carts are also used to travel short distances. Roads and railway tracks are built to help us travel on land.

Green Earth

Motor vehicles give out smoke, which makes the air dirty. We should walk or cycle or use a car pool to reduce smoke.

Vehicles move on land

We use boats, ships and other kinds of vehicles to travel by water.

Travel by water

We use an aeroplane, a helicopter and a hot air balloon to travel by air. Many people going to the same place can travel together in an aeroplane.

Travel by air

FACT CHECK

Rockets are tall and round spacecrafts that are used to travel to space.

Apply it!

Name five vehicles that you see on your way to school.

Skill Builder

Critical thinking skills: What is a cable car? Does it have wheels?

Problem solving skills: Mia and her neighbourhood friend go to the same school. Yet, both of them travel in different cars. Do you think this is right? What do you think Mia should do?

Life skills: What should we use to wash our cars? Discuss in the class.

1. Water from the hosepipe ☐
2. Water in a bucket ☐

Wind up

- We often go from one place to another for different work. This is called travelling.
- We travel by land, water and air to go to different places.
- We use different kinds of vehicles to travel.

Exercises

A. Choose the correct option to fill in the blanks.

1. A .... is a vehicle.
   a. bus b. air c. road
2. A .... can be used to travel short distances.
   a. cycle rickshaw b. train c. helicopter
3. A .... is mostly used in villages.
   a. bullock cart b. ship c. aeroplane
4. We use a .... to travel by water.
   a. bicycle b. boat c. train
5. We use a .... to travel by air.
   a. helicopter b. car c. ship
6. Many students together travel in a .... to their school.
   a. hot air balloon b. bus c. bicycle

B. Tick the vehicles in which you have travelled.

1. Bicycle ☐ 2. Car ☐ 3. Bus ☐

4. Train ☐ 5. Airplane ☐ 6. Rickshaw ☐

C. Look at the vehicles and circle them in different colours. Use red for air transport, blue for water transport and green for vehicles that travel on land.

Think Big

Crafts Fun

Make your own sailboat.

Material required: paper, ice cream sticks, a round plastic lid, water and play doh.

Method:

1. Cut out a coloured sheet of paper in the shape of a triangle and decorate it.
2. Take an ice cream stick and paste the triangle to form your mast.
3. Now, take a round plastic dish or lid and place a ball of play doh on it.
4. Fix the stick in the play doh and your sail boat is ready. The boat can also float in water.

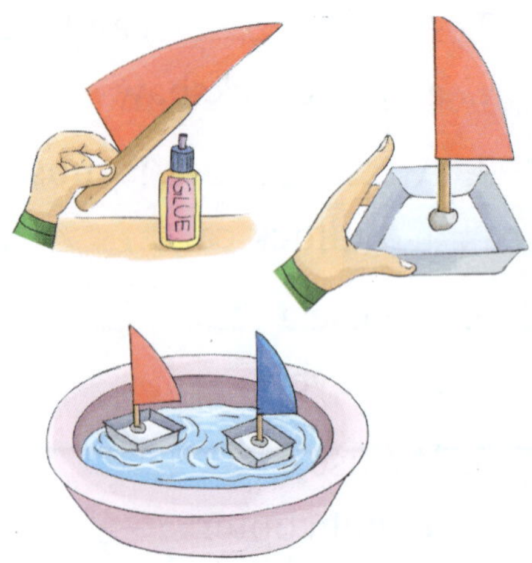

Learning Tools

Look at the pictures and solve the crossword. One has been done for you.

Web links:

https://www.india.gov.in/topics/travel-tourism/modes-travel
https://kids.nationalgeographic.com/search?q=transport&location=srp&type=manual

Last accessed on 30 August 2021

12. Be Safe

Warm up

Read the statements and take the 'be safe' quiz. Say yes or no.

1. Our home keeps us safe from rain.
2. Clothes keep us safe from insect bites.
3. Wearing a mask keeps us safe from falling sick.

Safety

Safety is being safe from **danger** or harm. We should always be careful and safe. To be safe, we need to follow certain rules. These rules help us avoid **accidents**. If we do not follow safety rules, we can hurt not only ourselves but others too.

Being Safe at Home

- Do not play with sharp things, such as scissors and knives, as they might hurt you and others. If you do need to use them, always ask an adult to help you.
- Do not play with electrical switches and plugs.
- Do not take medicines without taking permission from elders or a doctor.
- Do not go near the gas stove, oven or iron as you might get burnt from them.
- Do not play with matchsticks and candles.
- Do not open the door to **strangers**.

Use scissors with an adult

Do not open door to strangers

danger: a person or thing that may cause injury or pain; accident: an event that happens suddenly causing people harm; strangers: people you do not know

Apply it!

Circle the sharp things that we should not play with.

FACT CHECK

The red light says 'stop'.
The yellow light says 'wait'.
The green light says 'go'.

Being Safe on the Road

- Always wait for the traffic light to turn red and the traffic to stop before crossing the road.
- Always look at both the sides of the road before crossing.
- Cross the road only at the **zebra crossing**.
- While walking on the road, always walk on the **footpath**.
- While travelling in a car or a bus, never put your hands or head out of the window.
- Always wear a seatbelt while travelling by car and a helmet while riding a bike or a cycle.

Crossing a road

Standing in a queue

Being Safe at School

- Do not jump on desks and chairs.
- Do not push anyone while walking or climbing the stairs.
- Always stand in a queue while **boarding** and getting off a bus.
- In the playground, do not stand in front of swings or jump off seesaws.

Green Earth

Walk or use bicycle for short distances.

What's in the picture?

Name these objects that keep us safe.

LI...EB... ...Y FA.... ..... M....S.... S....A.... ....E....T ....E....M...T

zebra crossing: an area on the road painted with white stripes; footpath: a narrow path for walking; boarding: to get on to a bus or any other vehicle

First aid

First aid is the first help given to someone who is injured. We must keep a first-aid kit at home, in school and in the car.

Skill Builder

Critical thinking skills:

1. Look at the picture and say whether this action is safe or not. Talk about it in your class.
2. Where is it safe to play—in the classroom or in the playground? Why?

Life skills:

Your brother fell down and hurt himself. Tick (✓) what you would do.

1. Help him to get up. ☐
2. Start crying. ☐
3. Tell an adult to come and help. ☐

Wind up

- We should always be careful and take care of ourselves.
- We should protect ourselves from danger and harm to avoid accidents.
- To be safe, we must follow certain rules.
- We should follow the safety rules at home, on the road and in the school.

Exercises

A. Choose the correct option to fill in the blanks.

1. I .... play in the kitchen.
   a. do b. do not c. sometimes
2. I .... put my finger in an electrical socket.
   a. do b. do not c. often
3. I play in the ....
   a. park b. road c. balcony
4. The red traffic light means ....
   a. go b. stop c. wait

B. Write Y for the correct action and N for the wrong action.

C. Answer these questions.

1. Which objects should you not play with?
2. What does one wear while cycling?
3. What do you call the first help given to an injured person?

Think Big

English Fun

Find the words in the word grid with the help of picture clues.

S	T	E	T	H	O	S	C	O	P	E
W	I	R	U	P	A	Z	S	N	B	M
E	S	Y	R	I	N	G	E	J	A	E
D	V	G	T	L	A	H	M	P	M	P
O	I	F	M	L	G	O	I	Y	B	L
C	R	D	A	P	K	Z	X	K	U	A
T	U	H	O	S	P	I	T	A	L	S
O	S	L	K	N	L	A	U	O	A	T
R	Q	M	A	S	K	T	R	L	N	E
V	X	C	I	P	C	L	E	H	C	R
T	H	E	R	M	O	M	E	T	E	R

Learning Tools

Read the sentences with pictures of things in a first aid box you would have seen at home. Tick (✓) the correct ones. Take help of your parents.

I apply

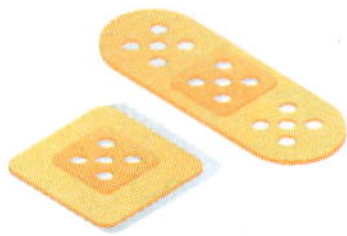

plaster | when I get hurt

I use

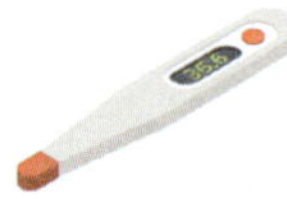

a thermometer | to cure my tummy

I have to

drink medicine | when I fall sick

My mother

wears gloves | to clean my wound

I clean my face

with a sanitizer | after playing

The doctor

ties a bandage | when my tooth aches

Web links:

https://www.education.com/resources/?q=safety

Last accessed on 30 August 2021

WORKSHEET

Worksheet (Chapters 9-12)

A. Choose the correct option to fill in the blanks.

1. We have .... meals in a day.
   a. two b. three c. five
2. Sometimes, a group of people wear special clothes called ....
   a. dress b. suit c. uniform
3. People eat community meals together in a ....
   a. langar b. hotel c. cafe
4. Any vehicle that one can travel or carry goods in is a means of ....
   a. work b. transport c. play
5. .... is being safe from danger or harm.
   a. Sleep b. Safety c. Travel
6. Many people going to the same place can travel together in an ....
   a. bicycle b. aeroplane c. hot air balloon
7. On Independence Day, the national flag is hoisted at the ....
   a. India Gate b. Red Fort c. National Stadium

B. Write L for land transport, W for water transport and A for air transport vehicles.

1. 

2. 

3. 

4. 

5. 

6. 

C. Write T for true and F for false sentences.

1. We must eat junk food. ....
2. We must not play on the road. ....
3. We should not open doors for strangers. ....

13. Plants Around Us

Warm up

Do you look at the plants and flowers in the park?

Do you like to see flowers in different colours? Can you identify any two plants in this garden?

Plants are all around us. We find them in gardens, in forests and even by the road. They are **living things**.

Types of Plants

Tree

Plants are different in shape, size and colour. Some are big, and some are small.

Plants that are big and tall are called trees. They have a strong, thick stem called trunk.

Shrub

Shrubs are the plants that are taller than herbs and shorter than trees. They have many branches and **woody** stems.

Short plants with soft, green stems are called herbs.

Climber

Herb

Some plants cannot stand straight and need some **support** to climb. They are called climbers.

Some plants **creep** on the ground. They are called creepers. Since their fruits are big and heavy, they spread their branches on the ground.

Creeper

living things: things that live and grow; woody: thick, hard and wood-like; support: to help something; creep: to move slowly, grow along the ground

Parts of a Plant

Look at the picture of the plant and read the names of its parts.

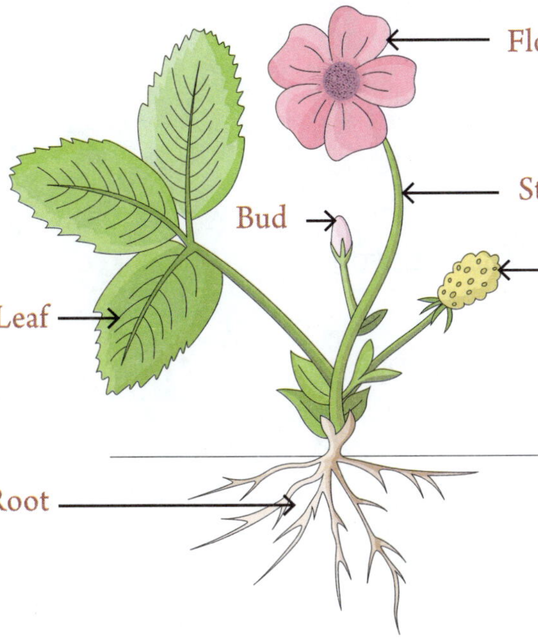

Parts of a plant

FACT CHECK

Plants need air, water, sunlight and soil. They can make their own food.

Green Earth

Trees are cut down to make paper. Therefore, we should not waste paper.

What's in the picture?

Look at the pictures. Name the part of the plant they belong to.

....

Uses of Plants

Plants are very useful to us. They give us:

- food such as fruits, vegetables, grains and leaves.
- wood which is used to make tables and chairs.
- materials such as cotton and jute that is used to make clothes and bags.
- medicines that come from leaves and flowers of some plants.

Plants keep the air we breathe fresh and clean. We should plant more trees and take care of them.

Apply it!

Circle the things that we get from plants.

Skill Builder

Critical thinking skills: Why do people cut trees? What will you do if you see someone cutting a tree?

Life skills: Imagine you are a plant and someone wants to adopt you. Write a list of instructions for your new owner, explaining how he or she should care for you.

Communicative skills: Make a poster on 'Plant more trees'.

Wind up

- Plants are living things.
- There are different kinds of plants such as trees, herbs, shrubs, climbers and creepers.
- Plants have many different parts.
- Plants are very useful to us.

Exercises

A. Look at the pictures. Tick (✓) the correct answers to name the type of these plants.

1. 
   a. Climber b. Herb
2. 
   a. Creeper b. Shrub
3. 
   a. Tree b. Climber

B. Match the columns.

	Column A		Column B
1.	Tree	a.	A short plant with soft green stems
2.	Herb	b.	Takes support to grow upwards
3.	Shrub	c.	Grows along the ground
4.	Creeper	d.	Shorter than trees and taller than herbs
5.	Climber	e.	Strong thick trunk

C. Answer these questions.

1. Name any three types of plants.
2. Name any four parts of a plant.
3. Name any three things that we get from plants.

Think Big

Data Fun

Look at the pictograph Azi had made listing the favourite fruit of her friends. Make a similar one for ten of your classmates.

Fruits	Number of students
Apple	
Orange	
Mango	
Banana	
Strawberry	

Learning Tools

Make a flower painting!

Material required: white sheet, paints, brush and crumpled newspaper

Method:

1. Dip crumpled newspaper ball in paint and make prints on white paper.
2. Now, paint the leaves and stalk of the flower with green paint and a paint brush.
3. Your flower painting is ready!

Web links:

https://www.nationalgeographic.org/education/resource-library/?q=plants&page=1&per_page=25
https://www.dkfindout.com/uk/search/plants/

Last accessed on 30 August 2021

14. Animals Around Us

Warm up

Which animal do you see in the picture? What sound does he make?

What is so special about this animal?

We can see many animals around us. Some animals are big and some are small. Birds, fish and insects are types of animals too.

Types of Animals

Some animals live with us in our homes. They are like our friends. We call them **pets**. Dogs, cats, and fish are some animals we keep as pets. We love and take care of our pets.

Pet animals

We keep some animals near our homes or on a farm as they are useful to us. We call them **domestic** animals. Horses, cows, buffaloes, camels and goats are some domestic animals.

Domestic animals

pets: animals we keep at home; domestic: not wild, animals kept at home or on a farm

Some animals live in forests. They are called wild animals. Lions, tigers, crocodiles and bears are some wild animals.

Wild animals

Apply it!

Find out more about any one pet, domestic and wild animal. Write a sentence about each.

1. Pet animal ....
2. Domestic animal ....
3. Wild animal ....

Food for Animals

Like human beings, animals also need food to live and grow. Different animals eat different kinds of food.

FACT CHECK

Plant-eating animals are called herbivores and flesh-eating animals are called carnivores.

Giraffe

Animals such as cows, goats, sheep, horses, elephants, giraffes and rabbits eat plants, fruits and vegetables.

Animals such as tigers, lions, foxes, eagles, cheetahs and wolves eat the flesh of other animals.

Animals such as bears, crows, dogs and cats eat both plants and the flesh of other animals.

Baby animals get their food from their mothers.

What's in the picture?

Look at the pictures and write the names of these animal babies.

....

Animal Homes

Different animals have different kinds of homes to protect them from rain, cold, heat and wind.

Birds make nests.

Fish is kept in an aquarium.

A cow lives in a shed.

Green Earth

Many animals are homeless. We must try to help them.

A horse lives in a stable.

A lion lives in a den.

A rabbit lives in a burrow.

Caring for Animals

Animals help us in many ways. We should take care of them. We must not trouble any animal.

We must look after animals

Skill Builder

21ST CENTURY SKILLS

Thinking skills: Solve these riddles.

1. I am the king of the jungle .... (OINL)
2. I have a long trunk .... (LEEPAHTN)
3. I am the tallest animal in the jungle .... (FFGRIAE)
4. I am the fastest animal .... (AHCEETH)

Life skills: Imagine you have a pet who falls sick. How would you take care of it with the help of your parents?

Wind up

- Pets live with us in our homes.
- Domestic animals are useful to us.
- Wild animals live in forests.
- Animals need food to live and grow.

Exercises

A. Look at the animals given here. Write whether they are pets or wild or domestic animals.

 ....
 ....
 ....
 ....
 ....
 ....

B. Match the animals and their homes.

	Column A		Column B
1.	Dog	a.	Burrow
2.	Birds	b.	Kennel
3.	Lion	c.	Den
4.	Horse	d.	Nest
5.	Rabbit	e.	Stable

C. Write T for true and F for false.

1. Crocodile is a wild animal. ☐
2. Giraffes eat plants and leaves. ☐
3. Lions and tigers eat flesh of other animals. ☐
4. We should take care of our pets. ☐

Think Big — Craft Fun

Let us make a toilet roll mouse.

Material required: toilet paper roll, coloured paper—grey, pink and white, black marker, glue and scissors

Method:

1. Take a toilet paper roll. Wrap grey paper around it and paste it.
2. Draw the nose and mark eyes on either side and draw the mouth.
3. Place a white circle below the mouth and paste in place to form the mouse's belly.
4. Cut out the ears and colour them pink on the inside and grey on the outside.
5. Glue them to the roll. Your cute mouse is now ready to squeak!

Learning Tools

1. Match the animals with their favourite food. One has been done for you.

2. Help the cow reach its shed.

Web links:

https://kids.nationalgeographic.com/nature/habitats
https://www.worldwildlife.org/habitats

Last accessed on 30 August 2021

15. Air and Water

Warm up

You would have seen the leaves of a tree moving or papers flying under a fan.

- What do you blow into a balloon?
- What makes the leaves of a tree move and fall?

Air and water are very important for all living things. We need air as well as water to live.

Air

Air is all around us. We cannot see air but we can feel it. We feel air when leaves rustle and when the fan gives a cool effect.

Air moves from one place to another. Moving air is called wind. When air moves softly, it is called a breeze. At times, the wind blows strongly. It is called a storm.

Try pinching your nose for a few seconds. Does that make you feel uneasy?

We need air to breathe and live.

FACT CHECK

We should plant more trees. Trees clean the air.

Uses of Air

Air is used by us in many ways. Air helps things, such as kites and aeroplanes, fly.

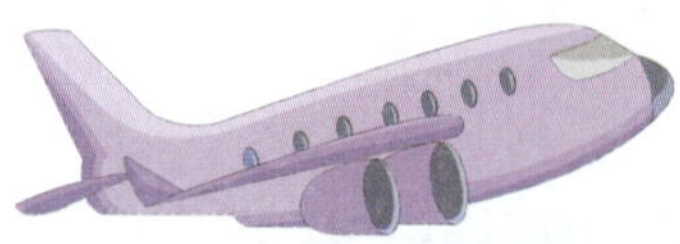

Air is needed to fill up flat tyres, balloons and footballs.

Air helps in drying wet clothes.

Air helps to start a fire.

Sailboats and windmills move with the help of air.

Can you think of some other uses of air?

Apply it!

Circle the things that need air to move.

Clean Air

We should keep the air clean. Smoke and dust make the air dirty. If we breathe dirty air, we will fall sick.

Smoke makes air dirty

Water

We need water to live, likewise the plants and animals need water to live. We require water for many activities in our daily life.

FACT CHECK

When we blow air into soapy water through a straw, we get **bubbles**.

Uses of Water

Green Earth

Do not waste water. Use only as much water as you need.

We all use water in many ways. We need water for drinking, bathing, cleaning and cooking. We also need water for putting out fires.

We use water for fun activities such as swimming and surfing.

Animals and birds also need water to drink and to keep their bodies cool.

bubble: a round ball of liquid, containing air, produced by soap and water

What's in the picture?

Tick (✓) the activities that require water.

Sources of water

We get water from **oceans**, seas, rivers, lakes, **streams**, ponds, handpump, wells and rain. These are known as the **sources** of water. We have pipes and taps in our homes that help us get water.

Lake

Well

River

Pond

Handpump

Ocean

Clean Water

We should always drink clean water. Drinking dirty water can make us fall sick. Animals and birds too can fall sick if they drink dirty water.

We should never throw garbage into lakes, rivers and other sources of water.

ocean: a very big amount of water in one place; stream: a small, narrow river; sources: a place, person or thing from which we get something

Skill Builder

Critical thinking skills: Tick (✓) what you would do in this situation.

You see that one of the taps in your house is leaking.

1. Tell your parents immediately. ☐
2. Try to fix it yourself. ☐
3. Let it leak. ☐

Life skills: Circle the people who are not dirtying the air.

Wind up

- Human beings, plants and animals need air and water to live.
- Air and water are useful in many ways.
- We should keep the air clean.
- We get water from many sources.
- Dirty water can make us sick.
- We should not waste water or make it dirty.

Exercises

A. Choose the correct option to fill in the blanks.

1. We can .... air.

   a. feel   b. see   d. smell

2. We need air to start a ....

   a. match   b. fight   c. fire

3. We should .... the taps after using them.

   a. turn on   b. turn off   c. throw

4. We should not drink .... water.

   a. clean   b. dirty   c. fresh

5. We get water in our homes with the help of ....

   a. pipes   b. ocean   c. bucket

6. We need air for ....

   a. cooking   b. breathing   c. swimming

B. Tick (✓) the things that can be done to keep the air and water clean.

1. Burn leaves and crackers ☐
2. Plant trees ☐
3. Never throw garbage in a river, lake or sea ☐
4. Walk for short distances ☐

C. Give two names for the following.

1. Things we fill with air ....
2. Things that move with the help of air ....
3. Sources of water ....
4. Uses of water ....

Think Big

Craft Fun

Let us make a wind chime.

Material required: five long sticks, five strings of equal length and one thick bangle

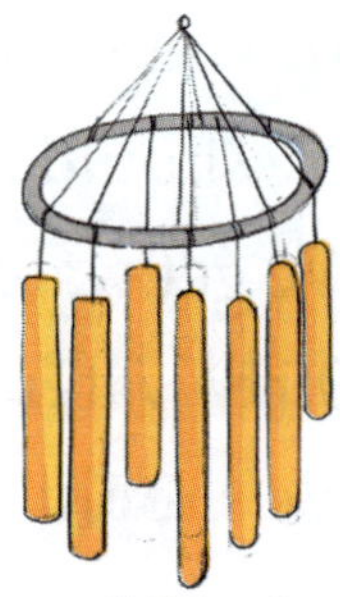

Method:

1. Take the sticks and tie each of them to separate strings.
2. Then tie the other end of the strings to the bangle.
3. Now tie a long string at the centre of the bangle which would help to hang the chime.
4. Your wind chime is ready!

Learning Tools

1. List three uses of water and of air in the boxes given below.

Uses of water	Uses of air
....	....
....	....
....	....

2. Help the boy reach the free ring.

Web links:

https://kids.nationalgeographic.com/search?q=Water&location=srp&type=manual
https://www.ducksters.com/science/environment/

Last accessed on 30 August 2021

16. Earth and Sky

Warm up

What do you see when you look up at the day sky?

The Earth is our home. It is round in shape like an orange. Land and water form our Earth. We live on the land along with many plants and animals. Fish, whales, tortoises and other animals along with some plants live in water.

Land

Land has many shapes and forms. It can be flat or raised. A flat land is called a plain. A raised land is called a hill. A high hill is called a mountain.

Land

Water

Water on the Earth is found in oceans, seas, lakes, rivers, ponds, springs, streams and waterfalls. In cold areas, water is found in the form of snow and ice.

Water

Apply it! E

Name two animals that you see:

On land ....

In water ....

In the sky ....

Green Earth

Always throw waste in a dustbin and do not dirty land or water.

FACT CHECK

Earth from space looks very colourful. We can see blue water, white clouds and brown and green land!

Sky

What do we see when we look up?

Day and night sky

The big open space above us is called the sky. It appears blue in the morning. We see the Sun and clouds in the sky during the day. The Sun gives light to the Earth. We can not directly look at the Sun as it hurts our eyes.

When the Sun goes down, it becomes the night. The sky appears dark blue in the night. We see stars and the moon in the night sky.

What's in the picture?

....

Look at these objects and say whether you see them at night or during the day.

Skill Builder

21ST CENTURY SKILLS

Critical thinking skills: Why does the sky turn dark at night?

Life skills: The Earth is beautiful, but we are making it dirty. We should keep the Earth clean. How can we keep it clean?

Collaborative skills: Discuss at least two ways in which you could help to keep our land and water clean.

Wind up

- The Earth is made up of land and water.
- The land has many shapes and forms.
- The sky has clouds, stars, the Sun and the moon.

Exercises

A. Choose the correct option to fill in the blanks.

1. In cold areas, water is found in the form of .... and ....
   a. river and pond   b. snow and ice
2. .... and .... can be seen in the sky at night.
   a. Moon and stars   b. Cars and kites
3. The Earth has both land and ....
   a. sky   b. water
4. A high hill is called a ....
   a. top   b. mountain

B. Match the columns.

	Column A		Column B
1.	Fish	a.	Plains
2.	Sun	b.	Snow
3.	Water	c.	Day
4.	Clouds	d.	Ocean
5.	Flat land	e.	Sky

C. Colour the picture.

Think Big

Number Fun

Count the number of objects you see outside during the day.

Learning Tools

Spot five differences in both the pictures.

Web links:

https://www.nasa.gov/kidsclub/index.html
https://www.dkfindout.com/uk/search/sky/

Last accessed on 30 August 2021

HC

What is happiness?

Happiness is a combination of feeling good and satisfied with your day.

Let us do some fun activities.

A. Sing 'Simon says' song with actions to remember the body parts. Take turns to be the leader, Simon!

Simon says raise your hands.
Simon says tap your feet.
Simon says close your eyes.
Simon says feel your hair.
Simon says touch your nose.
Simon says rub your knees.

B. Let us play the game of snakes and ladders to learn about good and bad habits. Watch out for the snakes!

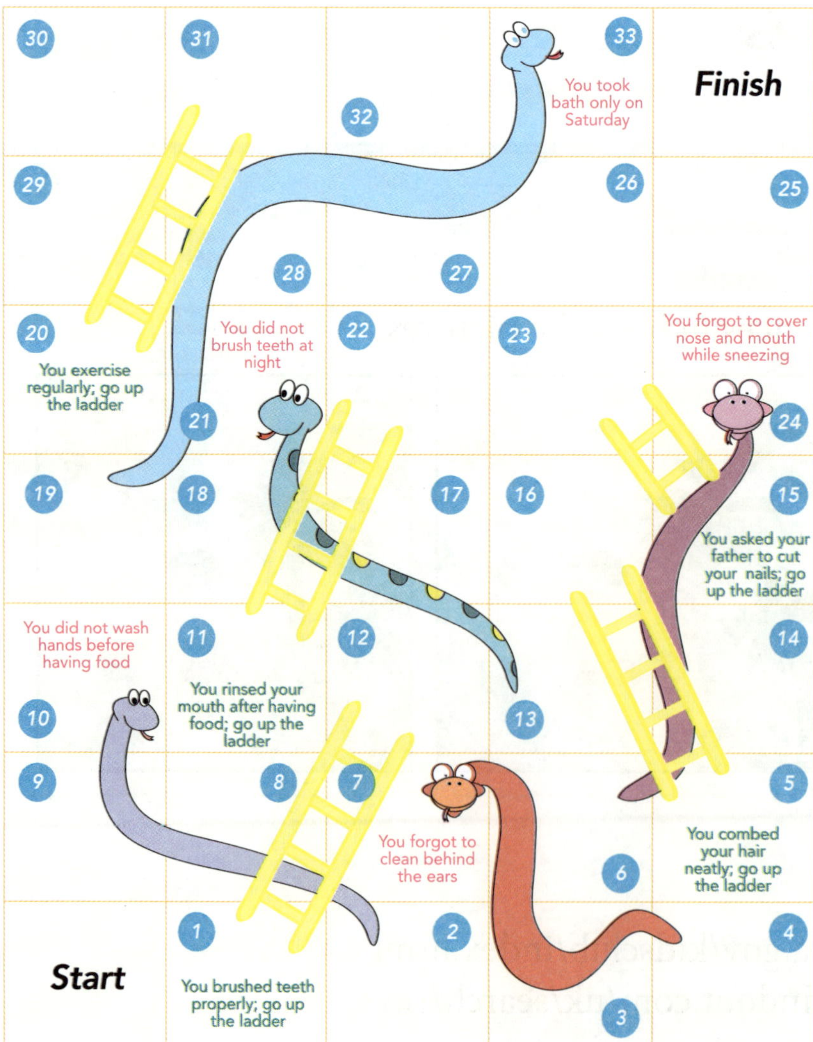

C. Look at the different colours given below. Colour the picture according to the correct number.

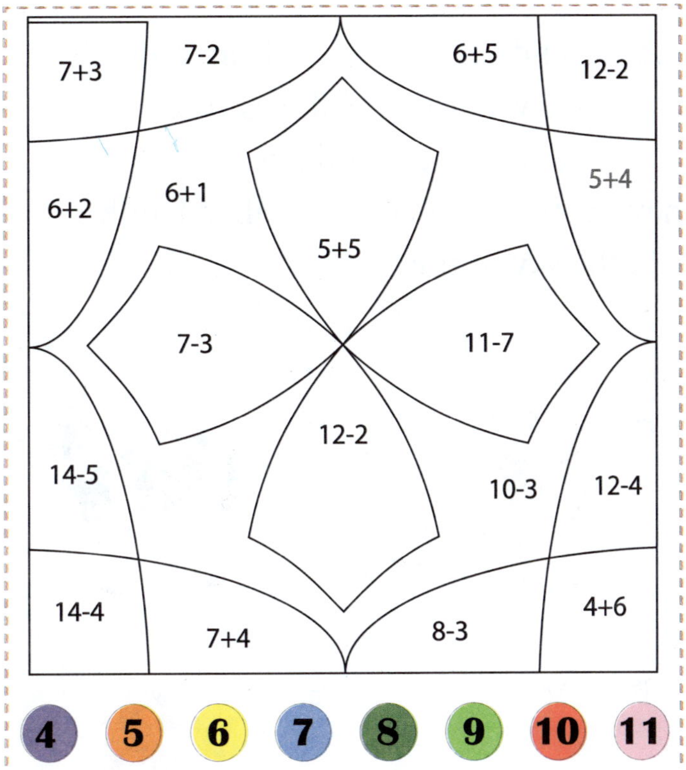

D. Help the four animals reach their homes.

WORKSHEET

Worksheet (Chapters 13-16)

A. Fill in the blanks.

1. We get .... and .... from animals.
2. Drinking .... water will make us sick.
3. We need .... to breathe and live.
4. .... have a strong, thick stem called trunk.
5. The Sun is high in the sky in the ....

B. Match the animals with the food that they like to eat.

1. 
2. 
3. 
4. 

a. 
b. 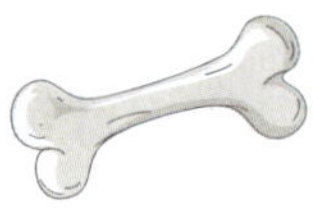
c. 
d. 

C. Write T for true and F for False.

1. Land has many forms. ☐
2. Air helps in drying wet clothes. ☐
3. We should never throw garbage in any source of water. ☐
4. Shrubs are taller than herbs and shorter than trees. ☐
5. The Sun rises in the evening. ☐

D. Where do you see these things? Write L for land, S for sky and W for water.

 ☐  ☐  ☐  ☐  ☐  ☐  ☐  ☐  ☐

ASSESSMENT 1

A. Choose the correct option to fill in the blanks.

1. We live with our ....
   a. friends b. family c. neighbours
2. We use our hands to ....
   a. write b. kick c. run
3. We must wear a mask while going out as it protects us from ....
   a. rain b. sun c. germs
4. Our classrooms should be ....
   a. dusty b. clean c. dark
5. A .... looks after us when we are sick.
   a. cleaner b. maid c. nurse

B. Write T for true and F for false sentences.

1. An identity card tells us nothing about the person wearing it. ☐
2. Exercise keeps us fit for the whole day. ☐
3. We must share work with our family members. ☐
4. We can throw papers in the classroom. ☐
5. Houses can be kutcha or pucca. ☐

C. Unscramble the words and write the correct words.

1. HBYBO ....
2. ENREYG ....
3. TGENOU ....
4. FMALIY ....
5. PMNOTAS ....
6. KTHCIEN ....

D. Match the following.

	Column A		Column B
1.	Doctor	a.	School
2.	Classroom	b.	Hospital
3.	Parents	c.	Write
4.	Park	d.	Family
5.	Hands	e.	Play

ASSESSMENT 2

A. Choose the correct option to fill in the blanks.

1. Children wear uniform in a ....
   a. restaurant b. school c. park
2. We decorate a tree to celebrate the festival of ....
   a. diwali b. gurpurab c. christmas
3. The .... makes the day warm and bright.
   a. star b. Sun c. moon
4. We need .... to put out fire.
   a. water b. air c. Sun
5. Plants give us .... to make table and chair.
   a. oil b. spices c. wood
6. .... animals live with us at home.
   a. Pet b. Farm c. Wild

B. Answer in one word.

1. This is all around us. ....
2. This animal lives in water. ....
3. I give heat and light to all. I am a big ball of fire. ....
4. I use this to talk to my friends and family members ....
5. It is a type of transport, it has two wheels, pedals and a handlebar. ....

C. Write Y for yes and N for No.

1. A clinic is bigger than a hospital. ☐
2. Trains can run on the road. ☐
3. Some vegetables can be eaten uncooked. ☐
4. We must cross the road at zebra crossing. ☐
5. Medicines must be taken with permission of an adult. ☐

D. Draw an elephant as shown here.

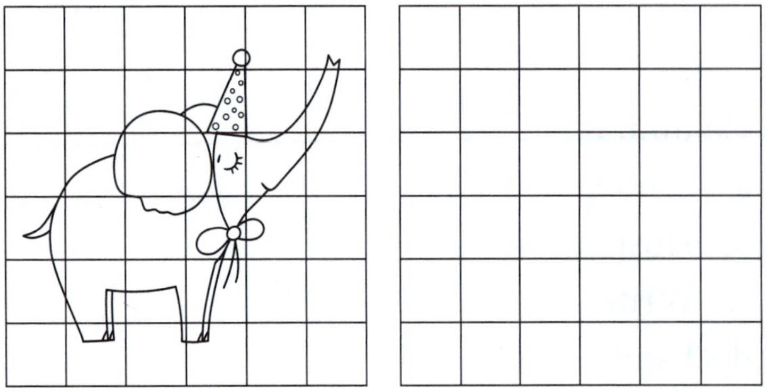